DOGS SET VI

MALTESE

Nancy Furstinger
ABDO Publishing Company

visit us at
www.abdopub.com

Published by ABDO Publishing Company, 4940 Viking Drive, Edina, Minnesota 55435.
Copyright © 2006 by Abdo Consulting Group, Inc. International copyrights reserved in
all countries. No part of this book may be reproduced in any form without written
permission from the publisher. The Checkerboard Library™ is a trademark and logo of
ABDO Publishing Company.

Printed in the United States.

Cover Photo: Corbis
Interior Photos: Animals Animals pp. 7, 19, 21; Corbis pp. 5, 11, 13, 15, 16, 17; Getty
    Images pp. 9, 12, 18

Series Coordinator: Megan M. Gunderson
Editors: Megan M. Gunderson, Megan Murphy
Art Direction: Neil Klinepier

Library of Congress Cataloging-in-Publication Data

Furstinger, Nancy.
    Maltese / Nancy Furstinger.
        p. cm. -- (Dogs. Set VI)
    Includes bibliographical references and index.
    ISBN 1-59679-272-8
        1. Maltese dog--Juvenile literature. I. Title.

SF429.M25F87 2005
636.76--dc22

                                                                                        2005043278

CONTENTS

THE DOG FAMILY

Dogs and humans have been living together for more than 12,000 years. People trained wolves as guards and hunters. Over time, these tamed animals became pet dogs. Early humans painted their dogs on cave walls around the world.

Today, about 400 dog **breeds** exist. Domestic dogs can range from pocket-size to pony-size. Some are still used to guard and hunt. Others were bred for different purposes, such as rounding up cattle and snuggling in laps.

All dogs belong to the Canidae **family**. Their close relatives include coyotes, foxes, jackals, and wolves. Today, they still share similar features, such as excellent smelling and hearing abilities.

Today, some dogs look more like their wolf relatives than others.

MALTESE

The Maltese **breed** dates back more than 2,800 years. These dogs were first brought to the Mediterranean island of Malta around this time.

Malta was a trading center between Africa and Europe. The island was influenced by Roman, Greek, Italian, French, British, and Arab travelers. The beauty and brains of the Maltese soon made them popular with many cultures.

Malta's Roman governor had a portrait painted of his Maltese, Issa. Greeks created tombs and artwork to honor their Maltese. Egyptians may also have worshipped them. In the 1500s, people paid large sums to own a Maltese.

In 1877, a Maltese was put on display at the Westminster Kennel Club Dog Show in New York City. This dog was listed as a Maltese Lion Dog. The Maltese **breed** was recognized by the **American Kennel Club (AKC)** in 1888.

In the past, Mediterranean travelers traded Maltese for Chinese silks and other valuable products.

What They're Like

Maltese crave attention. They are eager to play, and they quickly make new friends. They love to cuddle. And, they are known to charm themselves into the nearest lap. These affectionate dogs are clever and aim to please.

Despite their small size, Maltese are fearless and spirited. They usually bark at strangers. So, they make good watchdogs.

But if Maltese are **socialized** early, they will respond well to new people. Persistent training will prevent your pet from having undesirable manners.

Consistent training will help a Maltese learn which behaviors are acceptable in its new home.

COAT AND COLOR

Maltese have a soft, snow-white coat. They have been **bred** specifically to have a coat of only pure white. However, their ears can have a lemon or light tan tint.

Most dog breeds have an undercoat of shorter fur beneath the topcoat. Maltese only have the long topcoat. It flows flat almost to the ground.

The Maltese's tail is a long-haired sweep of fur that spills over the back. The tip of the tail lies just off to one side because of the weight of the fur.

Long fringes of hair feather the ears and head. Dark eyes sparkle in contrast to the spotless white coat. The hair is parted from the top of the Maltese's black nose to the base of its tail.

**This Maltese has a traditional look. However,
the short "pet trim" is easier to groom.**

SIZE

The Maltese is a tiny **breed**. In the 1600s and 1700s, these little pets could snuggle in a lady's sleeve. A woman in the 1800s would sometimes match her pet's hair ribbons to the color of her dress.

The Maltese's body is about as long as it is tall. Maltese stand six to seven

Maltese move gracefully in dog shows.

inches (15 to 18 cm) tall at the shoulders. They should weigh less than seven pounds (3 kg). The ideal weight is four to six pounds (2 to 3 kg). They move with a lively step on strong legs.

Maltese make great companion dogs.

CARE

Maltese need daily brushing. They also need a bath at least once every month to keep their silky coat gleaming. Otherwise that splendid fur will become a tangled mess!

Start grooming your Maltese as a puppy so that it gets used to the process. Use a brush and a comb made specifically for dogs. Slowly work your way through the coat using long strokes. A spray-on conditioner can help protect the fur.

As a finishing touch, add a topknot with bows. This will help keep the fur out of the Maltese's face. When you groom your Maltese, it will be happier and healthier.

After you, your dog's next best friend is the veterinarian. During an annual checkup, your Maltese will be examined and receive **vaccinations**. Your veterinarian can also **neuter** or **spay** your pet.

A ribbon is typically used to help tie up hair in a topknot.

FEEDING

Make sure your new Maltese arrives with a bag of its usual food. If you wish to switch, slowly mix in a new dog food. This will prevent your pet from getting an upset stomach.

Dogs require a balanced diet just like people do. Your dog's food should have a protein, such as chicken, listed as one of the first ingredients. Talk to your veterinarian if you are not sure your dog is getting the proper nutrition.

The feeding guide on the label lists how much to feed your dog

All dogs enjoy a healthy treat, especially as a reward for good behavior.

Some cities have stores that only sell food and treats for dogs!

based on its age and weight. Do not spoil your Maltese by overfeeding it. Excess weight can cause many different health problems.

Along with food, provide clean, fresh water in a bowl. Offer your dog a healthy treat or chew toy to keep its teeth clean. Try nylon bones, small raw carrots, or a squeaky toy.

THINGS THEY NEED

Maltese like a lot of attention. Give your pet plenty of cuddles. They love spending time with people. It's no wonder Maltese are sometimes called "the dog of a million kisses."

Maltese need to be socialized in order to behave well when meeting new dogs and people.

Maltese will go wherever you go. They love exercise and enjoy playtime in the park. Make sure your Maltese wears a collar. It should include your pet's name, address, and phone number. And, bring along a leash to keep your dog near you and safe.

After exercising, Maltese enjoy snoozing in a crate. This safe spot is similar to a wolf's den. The crate can act as a bed and a pet carrier. Be sure to include a dog toy to keep your pet company.

Maltese are small enough to be carried with you.

PUPPIES

A mother Maltese is **pregnant** for about nine weeks. Like other small **breeds**, there are usually between one and four puppies in each **litter**.

Newborn puppies spend most of their time sleeping. They cannot see, hear, or walk. Their eyes and ears open at around two weeks. Puppies start scampering about when they are three weeks old. They are usually **weaned** at six weeks.

Puppies can go to their new homes starting at around eight weeks of age. You can buy a **purebred** Maltese puppy from a responsible breeder. Or, you can adopt an adult dog from a breed rescue or the **Humane Society**.

After you bring home your Maltese, visit the veterinarian for a series of **vaccines**. Until it has its shots, keep your puppy safely away from other pets. A healthy Maltese will live about 12 to 15 years.

Getting a Maltese puppy is a big responsibility.

GLOSSARY

American Kennel Club (AKC) - an organization that studies and promotes interest in purebred dogs.

breed - a group of animals sharing the same appearance and characteristics. A breeder is a person who raises animals. Raising animals is often called breeding them.

family - a group that scientists use to classify similar plants or animals. It ranks above a genus and below an order.

Humane Society - an organization that protects and cares for animals.

litter - all of the puppies born at one time to a mother dog.

neuter (NOO-tuhr) - to remove a male animal's reproductive organs.

pregnant - having one or more babies growing within the body.

purebred - an animal whose parents are both from the same breed.

socialize - to accustom an animal or person to spending time with others.

spay - to remove a female animal's reproductive organs.

vaccine (vak-SEEN) - a shot given to animals or humans to prevent them from getting an illness or disease.

wean - to accustom an animal to eat food other than its mother's milk.

WEB SITES

To learn more about Maltese, visit ABDO Publishing Company on the World Wide Web at **www.abdopub.com**. Web sites about Maltese are featured on our Book Links page. These links are routinely monitored and updated to provide the most current information available.

INDEX